SHUTTING DOWN BULLIES

SHUTTING DOWN
SOCIAL BULLYING

Pam T. Glaser and Jason Porterfield

rosen publishing's
rosen
central

New York

Published in 2020 by The Rosen Publishing Group, Inc.
29 East 21st Street, New York, NY 10010

Copyright © 2020 by The Rosen Publishing Group, Inc.

First Edition

Library of Congress Cataloging-in-Publication Data

Names: Glaser, Pam T., author. | Porterfield, Jason, author.
Title: Shutting down social bullying / Pam T. Glaser and Jason Porterfield.
Description: New York : Rosen Publishing, 2020 | Series: Shutting down bullies |
Audience: Grade level 5–8. | Includes bibliographical references and index.
Identifiers: LCCN 2019011114| ISBN 9781725346956 (library bound) | ISBN 9781725346949 (pbk.)
Subjects: LCSH: Bullying—Social aspects—Juvenile literature.
| Bullying—Prevention—Juvenile literature.
Classification: LCC BF637.B85 G53 2019 | DDC 302.34/3—dc23
LC record available at https://lccn.loc.gov/2019011114

Manufactured in the United States of America

Some of the images in this book illustrate individuals who are models.
The depictions do not imply actual situations or events.

CONTENTS

Introduction

Social bullying occurs within a specific social circle. For young people, a social circle can include school, church, a sports team, work, or any similar group where certain people spend time together. Because social circles are such a big part of being a teen or preteen, social bullying is especially prevalent in their lives. That's why it's important to understand the different types of bullying and recognize when you, a friend, or someone else you care about is the victim of it.

One type of social bullying is social alienation, in which one individual is singled out from a group and made to feel alone. A group of friends may plan a party and purposefully exclude someone from the invite list. A bully may befriend a victim's BFF in an attempt to come between the friends and leave the victim friendless. The goal is to target one person and isolate him or her from others, either physically or socially.

Another type of social bullying is rumor spreading. A group of people might pass around damaging personal information about someone in a group text or on social media. They might even fabricate a rumor meant to make the target look bad and turn others against him or her.

There is often no reason for this kind of bullying, except that the target is different in some way. A bully or group of bullies often target someone because they want to improve their social standing in front of someone more popular. They might simply be bored. Bullies or groups of bullies make it difficult to break the cycle of abuse. People who step in and

Middle school and high school can be rough for a lot of young people, who have to deal not only with getting to class on time and homework, but social challenges, like bullying, too.

try to help might become victims themselves. Others know they should do something but want to avoid getting involved. Reporting the abuse to an authority figure might just add to the abuse. Some people in positions of power might see the bullying as harmless or just tell a victim to ignore it.

When a victim feels powerless, that feeling only spirals if nothing happens to change the situation. Bullying and social isolation can affect a student's grades, end a promising job prospect, cause long-term depression, or even make a person feel so hopeless that he or she considers or attempts suicide.

This type of bullying can be difficult to stop, especially if a person feels isolated and alone. But there are ways to get yourself out of a harmful situation and places to go for help.

CHAPTER ONE

Understanding Bullying

Lots of young people deal with bullying on a daily basis. Many don't even realize that what they're facing is bullying. Some people believe that if bullying doesn't involve violence, then it's just part of being a teen or preteen and is as easy to deal with as "walking away from the situation" or "being the bigger person."

BULLYING EXPLAINED

Bullying is unwanted, abusive behavior directed at a person by another individual or by a group of people. Usually, it is seen as a way to make the bully feel powerful while the bully's target feels weak.

Bullying can be physical, verbal, or psychological (when the bully uses ways to control or change a person's relationships with peers). Bullying can range from such behavior as name-calling or physical attacks to more subtle forms. Direct physical and verbal abuse are the most obvious forms of bullying and are also the forms that can most easily be combated by teachers, parents,

Lots of teens can feel isolated and ostracized by classmates and in social circles. Social alienation is often as difficult to face as more direct forms of bullying.

or friends. More subtle forms are harder to fight because they're harder to see.

Social alienation is one of these indirect types. Social alienation isolates a person from his or her peers and makes the bullying target feel alone. Physical bullying is not usually involved, although verbal bullying might be included.

With social alienation, the bully's target is deliberately left out of activities. The bullies may stop speaking to the bullied person or stop responding when he or she speaks. When the tar-

Long-term issues with social bullying can lead to depression for many teens.

get is there, the bullies may talk around him or her, making insulting or rude comments about the person as though he or she isn't present. When the bullied person tries to defend himself or herself, the bullies may ignore the target. The bullies may also pressure the target's friends into going along with the bullying. Electronic devices and social media can also be used to isolate and harass a bullied person.

Although bullies who take part in socially alienating behavior may not physically hurt the individual, their actions still cause harm. Any form of bullying damages the target's self-esteem. He or she may become lonely, anxious, and depressed. The bullied person's behavior may change. He or she may stop eating or eat more than usual. Sleep patterns may also change, with the victim getting too much or too little sleep. The stress of being bullied can affect a person's health. Bullied people have been found to get sick frequently. They may go out of their way to avoid the bullies, even cutting classes or avoiding school altogether.

People who face social alienation often start withdrawing from others. They may stop taking part in activities that they once enjoyed because they feel shut out. For example, an actor in a school play may quit the production because he or she feels isolated by the obvious and deliberate refusal of others to acknowledge his or her successes or offer comfort for failures. The bullies accomplish their goal as the socially alienated person becomes withdrawn.

HOW BULLYING CAN AFFECT YOU

Bullying can start at any point in school or in other social situations in which young people are in attendance. Children may start bullying others as early as age four, usually in quarrels over toys or taking turns. As they age, bullies may start to focus on wanting to get their own way. They threaten others while playing so that they succeed in getting what they want. By the time children reach the third grade, they start to focus on the idea of treating others fairly. At this point, bullies may start teasing other children or gossiping about them.

Some people become bullying targets very early in life. Once a pattern of bullying behavior is established, it can be hard to break. People can go through elementary school, middle school, and even high school as victims of the same bullies.

Other people may become bullying targets later, when they reach middle school or high school. They may start out with a lot of friends, do well in their classes, play sports, and be popular with their peers. However, this can all change if a person is bullied.

School sports teams are often a source of camaraderie for teens, but bullying can occur among teammates, too.

Targets for social alienation are often popular students who are doing well, such as in academics, music, or sports. The goal of the bully is to make the targeted person lose his or her sense of accomplishment and self-worth. The bully does this by isolating the target and pressuring others to do the same. The victim's accomplishments are diminished when he or she no longer gets respect and praise from others.

People who are bullied may be constantly battling low self-esteem. They lose confidence in their actions. They may feel that everything they do is wrong and that they are being criticized all the time. As the person's sense of self-worth declines and he or she withdraws, friends may start pulling away and stop offering their support.

Bullying is not limited to the school environment. Bullies can be found in study groups, parks, neighborhood settings, or any other social situation. Family members may bully other relatives. Even adults can be the victims of bullies at work.

THE HARM OF SOCIAL ALIENATION

All bullying is hurtful to the victim and to the bully. The pain caused by emotional bullying, such as social alienation, is harmful even if it does not leave physical marks. With social

MCKENZIE ADAMS

Nine-year-old McKenzie Adams enjoyed riding her bike and playing video games and wanted to be a scientist when she grew up. But for several months leading up to her death in December 2018, McKenzie had been dealing with bullying from some of her classmates at school. She had made friends with a classmate who was white (McKenzie was African American) and got a ride to school with the boy's family. McKenzie's family believes that this friendship made McKenzie a target of racist bullying. According to her family, one student kept writing McKenzie notes calling her names and telling her to kill herself. The family complained to the school board, but the harassment continued. McKenzie ultimately took her own life.

While many young people endure bullying without the crisis leading to suicide, mental health professionals believe that bullying in combination with a number of other factors can lead to suicidal ideation—contemplating or thinking about suicide—engaging in self-harm or suicidal acts, or even taking one's own life. Bullying can intensify already existing issues with anxiety, depression, or other mental disorders. If a young person can't find relief, he or she might feel like suicide is the only option.

alienation and other forms of emotional bullying, it can be hard to show that the bullying is occurring.

People who experience social alienation see their former friends stop interacting with them and perhaps even join the bullies. They may hear their peers gossiping about them or spreading rumors. However, when they try to defend themselves, the bullies ignore their protests and continue their harassing behavior.

If a large group is taking part in the bullying, it may seem impossible to escape the bullies. In school, a person may have to endure several classes throughout the day with their tormentors. It may even be difficult to get away from the bullies in clubs, sports, and after-school activities, depending on how widespread the social alienation becomes. Things that the bullied person took pride in, such as grades, friends, or a particular skill or talent, may become focal points for bullies.

The bullied individual may try turning to a friend, only to find that the friend is no longer interested in talking to him or her. The friend may believe that by hanging out with the target, he or she may also become bullied. A bullied person might find that no one wants to sit with him or her at lunch or on the bus. Free time during the school day may be hard for the bullied person to take, as other kids either ignore or harass him or her. After school and on the weekends, the bullies may reach out to harass their victim using text messages or social media.

The bullied person may attempt to make new friends, only to discover that no one wants to be his or her friend. The individual may give up on forming new friendships that could break the cycle of bullying.

One bullied girl, who told her story on AboutHealth.com, described how her friends on the cheerleading team turned against her because she didn't behave like them. The other girls would be rude or hurtful toward her until she didn't want to go to school. The bullied girl reported that she was able to overcome the bullying once she realized that they ganged up on her only as a group and that by themselves they didn't have the courage to tell her what they believed. She also had a caring family who offered encouragement.

A teen who deals with bullying might experience issues with minor to severe levels of anxiety.

BULLYING AND CONSEQUENCES

Unfortunately, the bullying that a person experiences at school can follow him or her into adulthood. People who are shunned, left out of social activities, or the victims of rumors in school remember this treatment, and it can seep into later relationships. Targets of social alienation often suffer from depression, anxiety, and feelings of loneliness in adulthood.

According to a Pew Research Center survey from 2018, 59 percent of US teens have been bullied or harassed online. Forty-two percent say they have been the victim of offensive name-calling, while 32 percent share that a bully has shared false information about them on the internet. Online harassment is on the rise, as new forms of communication continue to be developed. The effects of bullying, either online or offline, are known to be universally damaging, though. "Despite being an adult, I still bestow the scars from being tortured in my past," said author Alex S. in a post on the website Beyourself.

Where Bullies Come From

Bullies are individuals who engage in acts of harmful physical violence or harassment. People may begin bullying at any age, though the pattern of bullying is often set when the person is very young. Some bullies grow out of their behavior. Others continue to make their classmates, coworkers, and neighbors miserable throughout their lives.

WHY BULLY?

Bullying can have numerous causes, but it often stems from self-esteem issues. The bully behaves aggressively as a way to deal with his or her own lack of self-respect. By dominating others and possibly gaining the admiration of peers, the bully may feel more self-confident.

Some bullies act aggressively because of problems at home. They may be abused or mistreated by a parent, an older sibling, or a caregiver. By gaining power over others, they may feel that they are making up for their lack of power at home. Or if they are not abused, they may be emotionally neglected. Their parents, guardians, or caregivers may not pay enough attention to them. They may not actively abuse the bully, but emotional distance can also make a person feel unimportant.

Bullies can also be going through a rough time at home, even if there is no physical or emotional abuse. Any number of events within a family can set off bullying behavior. Maybe the bully has a new sibling and is feeling left out. Or the bully's parents are divorcing. Money problems or other troubles could put stress on the family's life and cause a child to bully peers.

Some bullies may have been bullied themselves. For them, bullying is a way to regain their social standing. Bullies often

Bullies often act out with bullying behavior because they themselves are experiencing abuse.

feel that their own social standing is low and so they feel isolated. They want to win approval from their friends and admiration from others. To do this, they pick targets that few of their peers would be willing to defend.

Bullies can be any gender. Bullies who are boys tend to engage in more physical and direct forms of bullying. Bullies who are girls are more likely to use indirect bullying tactics, such as social alienation.

HIDING IN PLAIN SIGHT

Successfully bullying someone may make a bully feel more confident. The bully may gain a sense of power over the target and a self-esteem boost from his or her friends. This is especially true of social alienation, in which the bully can act like a leader by getting others to isolate another person.

Electronic devices and social media can make it easier for bullies to isolate their targets without getting caught. Harassing messages can often be sent using false identities, although bullies may use their own names as a way to make their target feel more disconnected. A bully can also use technology to organize others into bullying the target.

As the bully gets more confident, he or she may push the victim harder. With social alienation, this means that the bully may pressure more people into isolating the bullied person through taunts, rumors, and other tactics. For the bully, there can never be too much pressure applied to the target. As the pressure on the bullying target increases, so does the pressure on others to take part in the hostility.

This is one reason why bullies are often able to get away with bullying behavior. People who want to defend the bullied individual may be discouraged from stopping or reporting the bullies. Instead, they become bystanders.

Bystanders may not like the bullying, but they do not act to stop it or attempt to befriend the bullied person. They may

Going along with bullying or not doing anything to put a stop to a friend's behavior may encourage a bully to continue doing harm to a victim.

be afraid that they will also become objects of bullying if they try to stop it, or they may already be bullied themselves. They may see the socially alienated person as one of the few peers who are more unpopular than they themselves are.

Social pressure from peers also stops many bystanders from telling an adult that the bullying is taking place. They may be afraid that they will be the next target or that they will be labeled as someone their peers can't trust and will be isolated, too.

The bullied person may also not want to tell an adult. That person may think that he or she will appear weak by telling adults about the bullying. People who are bullied may also be hesitant to tell someone about what is going on because they hope that the bullying will stop on its own. Or they may be afraid that it will get worse if they tell. With social alienation, bullies often choose people whom they envy to be their targets. The bully may hope to gain social status by finding a way to spoil the successes of their targets. The people bullies choose to target are often shy or lack confidence. They may not stand up for themselves or be able to find other ways to thwart the bully.

BREAKING THROUGH BULLYING BEHAVIOR

Bullies often struggle with their own issues of anger or lack of self-esteem. Often, they bully others because they feel helpless in other parts of their lives, and this behavior helps them to feel more in charge.

While it might seem like a bully's habits are permanent, it is possible to curb his or her behavior with the right resources and help. The first thing to do, if you're afraid you might be a bully, is to confront your own behavior. Are you causing harm to someone else either through physical violence, threats, or turning others against him or her? It's time to step away from the situation. Talk to a parent or trusted adult about your concerns. There might be counseling options available in your area. Learning ways to help deal with anger or feelings of inadequacy can do a lot to improve your self-worth. Get involved in a social group or new hobby or activity where you'll have a chance to make some new friends.

Even if the victims do tell, it can be hard to convince an adult that bullying is taking place. This is particularly true of social alienation because physical contact and verbal abuse aren't needed to isolate the victim. Teachers may not realize that a student is being socially alienated, or they may feel powerless to stop the behavior because no direct contact is taking place. Although they may be able to stop students from badgering or gossiping about their peers in class, they find it hard to stop someone from ignoring another person.

AS BULLIES GROW UP

Bullies don't necessarily remain bullies for their entire lives. Children who bully at a young age may grow out of the behavior as they mature. Those who start bullying as a way to deal with problems at home may stop once a situation has been resolved.

Many bullies grow into adulthood struggling with addictions to drugs and alcohol.

Some bullies never grow out of bullying. For these people, bullying may become so ingrained that they cannot stop. They learned that they could get what they wanted by bullying, so they never changed their behavior.

As these bullies grow older, some change their tactics. Bullies who were once more physical may become subtler. Instead of physically harassing their victims, they may engage in socially alienating tactics, such as spreading rumors or mocking the bullied person.

Long-term bullies may have other problems as well. Studies cited by the US government show that bullies are more likely to abuse alcohol and other drugs and have criminal convictions and traffic citations as adults. They are also more likely to be abusive toward their spouses, children, or other loved ones when they are adults.

However, it is never too late to stop bullying. One Reddit forum post asks "Former bullies of Reddit, are you sorry? Would you like to apologize to your victims?" and many commenters came forward with their own confessions of bullying behavior. Said one, "It wasn't until recently I kind of realized that I grew up in a pretty mentally abusive and physically abusive household. I guess when it comes down to it, I didn't really know how to be kind to other people, and I took out a lot of the frustrations from my home life on others." Another said, "I never bullied anyone, but my biggest regret from high school is that I rarely stuck up for the bullied." Adults often realize that their behavior as children or teens was problematic. Many seek out past victims and apologize, but the guilt may remain.

MYTHS AND FACTS ABOUT BULLYING

Myth: Bullies are always larger than their victims.

Fact: Bullies can be anyone, large or small, child or adult, who repeatedly engages in harassment or commits acts of violence against another individual. Your bully might be a family member, a classmate, a friend, or even an authority figure.

Myth: Bullying means causing physical harm to a target.

Fact: Bullying is not limited to acts of physical violence. Bullies can call a victim names, send harassing messages via social media, or start rumors. They can make threats of physical violence. Bullying can mean purposely leaving someone out of a fun activity as a way of hurting him or her.

Myth: Bullies are always boys.

Fact: Bullies can be any gender, and so can their victims. Boys are more likely to be victims of physical bullying, while girls struggle more often with psychological harm and teasing.

CHAPTER THREE

How to Escape and cope

Bullies are often portrayed as individuals with a physical advantage over their victims, but this is not always true. Bullying involves an imbalance of power between the bully and the bullied person. Sometimes the bully is the bigger or older of the two, but bullies can be physically smaller. Usually bullying victims have at least one characteristic that makes them stand out from or be rejected by the rest of their peers. This can be a physical characteristic, such as size, race, or the way the target talks, or it could be a personality trait. The bullied person could be extremely shy or socially awkward. A talent or particular skill that sets a person apart can lead to bullying, particularly if it is in an area that the bullies don't respect or in which the bully is jealous of the targeted victim's success.

HOW BULLIES CHOOSE VICTIMS

People chosen as bullying targets may have easygoing personalities that cause them to tolerate extreme behavior in others, or they may be unassertive and unwilling to defend themselves. They can be popular among some people and yet unpopular with others. Bullied people may not realize that they are disliked by a particular group until the bullying begins. With social alienation, the bullying can spread beyond the bully's friends until the targeted person is ignored by many other peers, including people they considered friends.

People who are different because of their race, religion, or sexual or gender identity are often the target of social alienation.

HOW TO COPE

It may seem easy to give in to bullying or tempting to fight back physically. Fighting back, however, may get the target in trouble and give the bully the moral high ground to continue the alienating behavior. On the other hand, the targeted person might think that if he or she does what the bully wants, the bully will stop the attacks.

With social alienation, bullied people may drop activities they once enjoyed, stop hanging out with people they considered friends, and withdraw in the classroom. They may start missing school as a way to avoid the pain of social alienation, causing their grades to suffer. In extreme cases, the person who is bullied may transfer to another school or even drop out of school to avoid bullies.

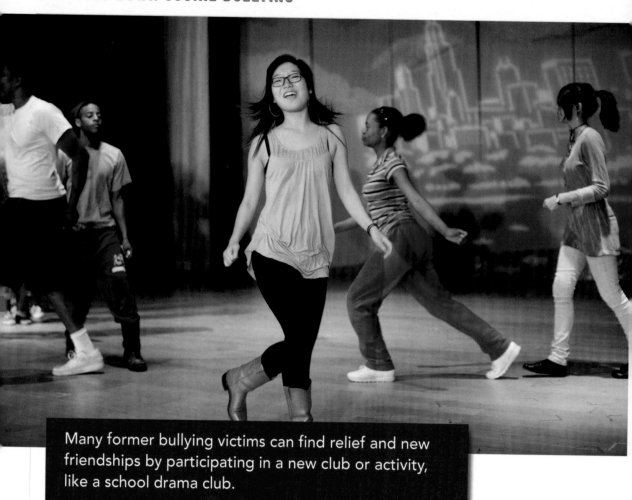

Many former bullying victims can find relief and new friendships by participating in a new club or activity, like a school drama club.

It takes work to escape a bully. A bullied person has to try to put the bullying aside. People who become socially alienated by bullying may have personality traits that must be overcome so that they can beat bullying. They may be too passive, anxious, insecure, or sensitive. Bullying can bring these traits out and hide positive aspects of a person's personality.

Regaining confidence can be an important first step. Social alienation often damages a person's confidence, especially the

SPEAKING TO A THERAPIST

Many young people might be nervous about speaking to a mental health professional because needing help implies there's something wrong with you. But there's nothing wrong or bad about seeking help if you're struggling. The experience can be very positive for both the victims of bullies and the bullies themselves. Therapists or counseling professionals work to help patients feel comfortable enough to share their feelings. They listen, offer input and advice, and help their clients develop an understanding of why they feel angry, sad, or helpless in certain situations. Therapists can also help young people develop strategies for coping with painful feelings or replacing addictive habits with healthier ones. Some therapists work one on one with patients, while others may coach a group therapy session. Discovering the best type of therapy for yourself is key.

Finding the right therapist or other mental health professional can be challenging. A parent or other trusted adult can help you to reach out for help if you feel you need it. Talk to a school guidance counselor if you don't feel you can get that kind of support at home. If you're afraid to ask for help from someone you know, reach out to a teen help line like TEEN LINE, YouthLine, The Trevor Project (for LGBTQ teens) or, if necessary, the Suicide Prevention Hotline. Calls are anonymous, and you can simply reach out and find someone to listen without being afraid of others finding out.

ability to make and keep friends. Bullied people have to make themselves visible in a positive way.

Bullied individuals who are already involved in school activities or sports should remain involved. Instead of focusing on the bullies, they might try to broaden their range of friends by hanging out with others who share their interests. The activity—whether it is music, sports, theater, clubs, or volunteer work—can help a bullied person take his or her mind off of the bullying. Getting to know new people involved in the same activity and becoming friends with them can help boost a person's self-esteem. Deep bonds can form between sports teammates or cast members working together to stage a play.

MAKING FRIENDS

Building successful relationships can help restore a bullied person's confidence. More important, close friends can help fight off the social alienation tactics used by bullies. With luck, finding a few close friends will lead to more friends, as those first friends introduce the bully's target to their other friends.

However, not every attempt to reach out to make friends will work. The bullied person may reach out and be turned away, sometimes over and over. The pattern of rejection can be discouraging, and the bullied person may want to give up.

Developing relationships takes work and time. The people whom the target approaches may be shy. If they know about the social alienation, they may be wary of becoming friends out of fear that they, too, will become the objects of bullying.

Making friends can be challenging for those who are shy or have felt ostracized in the past, but a new group of friends can make a big difference.

If a bully's target is involved in a team sport or group activity, he or she may have an easier time making friends with other participants because they already share at least one interest. The target should take the time to figure out who might have the qualities he or she wants in a friend. Is the person generally friendly? Does the prospective friend have a good sense of humor or share the target's interests? The person who is bullied should find someone who matches up well with his or her personality.

The bullied person should also take things slowly once he or she has figured out whom to befriend. Appearing overeager can drive a person away, but the target can't seem withdrawn or distant. If the potential new friend is someone the bullied person doesn't know well, he or she might begin with saying a simple hello and making small talk. There is nothing to lose by being friendly and polite. Even if the person does not want to become friends, he or she may remember the target as someone who is worthy of respect.

The bullied person should act confident when trying to make friends but avoid appearing overconfident. Some may be put off by someone who appears too cocky. It may be difficult to find the right balance between confidence and humility. If the target does something really well that earns praise from peers, such as playing a difficult solo, he or she should accept it gracefully, rather than brag about it. Be quick to praise others, but don't overdo it or it might seem as though the bullied person is trying to ingratiate himself or herself to others. If someone else helps the victim perform well, he or she should be sure that that person also gets credit. The other person will appreciate the acknowledgment of his or her role.

The bullied individual should try to stay positive and focus on social interactions that have gone well. He or she should be patient and keep trying. By making the effort, the bullied person can show that he or she is someone that others should want to get to know, rather than someone to ignore.

One way to show confidence is to be assertive in dealing with others. The bullied individual should suggest activities for his or her friends and take the first step in making connections.

Don't wait for friends to call, but call them first with a suggestion, such as going to a game or to the movies. If a friend calls you first, be ready to go out and have a positive attitude about what the activity might be, even if it is something that you have never tried.

Humor can also be used to make friends and to stump bullies. The bullying behavior may hurt deeply, but being able to laugh through the pain can confuse bullies. A sense of humor can also help a bullied person attract new friends. Others may come to admire a person who shows the inner strength to smile through a trying situation.

If it isn't possible to break the pattern of social alienation, it may be time to tell an adult. Parents or older relatives may not be able to help directly, but it can be comforting just to talk about one's problems.

Family members can help ease feelings of social alienation in more direct ways. Siblings or cousins close in age may be willing to hang out with the bullied person even when others aren't, even introducing them to their own friends and opening up the possibility of forming friendships away from the bullies. Older relatives can also help. They may be able to introduce the bullied person to volunteer opportunities or group activities where the individual can meet new people and make friends.

10 GREAT QUESTIONS
TO ASK A THERAPIST

1. What do I do when I feel like there's something wrong with me?

2. How can my parents help me to cope?

3. Why me?

4. What should I do if I'm afraid in school?

5. How can I cope with bullying that's happening at home?

6. How can I feel less alone?

7. What can I do if I'm having suicidal thoughts?

8. What's the best way to handle an immediate threat to my safety?

9. How can I deal with anger and other extreme emotions?

10. What can I do to break the bullying cycle?

CHAPTER FOUR

Coming Back

For a long time, bullying was written off as just a part of growing up. Children who were bullies were expected to grow out of bullying. Those who suffered the bullying were told to stand up for themselves and just get through it because the experience would help build character.

Today, bullying is more widely seen as a common problem found in schools, workplaces, and other settings. People don't often recognize social alienation as bullying unless they see it in the form of insults or gossip.

Bullying isn't limited to teenage years and school. Bullies exist in workplaces as well.

BREAKING OUT OF SOCIAL ALIENATION

Social alienation is a common result of many forms of indirect bullying. The damage caused by social alienation can be difficult to recognize. Bullying targets may avoid telling anyone about the situation. They may not ask for help in dealing with bullies because they are afraid of appearing weak and unable to handle their own problems. Although friends or family members may see that there is a problem, they may not know what is causing the bullied person to withdraw.

Even if parents and friends know about the social alienation happening at school, they may not be able to stop it. Many schools have policies against bullying, but they may not be broad enough to cover social alienation. After all, it is hard to crack down on students who ignore their peers. Teachers and administrators may know about it but are unable to make it stop.

There can be tremendous pressure not to report bullying. Bullies may threaten their targets and bystanders if their actions are reported. Many targets do not report bullying because they don't want to make the situation worse by angering the bully.

BULLYING AND SUICIDE

Some people may be able to ignore the bullying so successfully that the bullies give up. Other bullied individuals may take years to get over their mistreatment. Some never fully recover their confidence. Those who have been socially alienated may be extremely uneasy in social situations later in life, or they may completely avoid social activities.

COPING AS AN LGBTQ INDIVIDUAL

More and more teens and preteens are coming to terms with their unique gender or sexual identity at an earlier age than many did in the past, and this can make school or other social situations pretty difficult. The important thing to remember is that you have as much right to attend school in safety as any student. You might discover that you aren't alone in your identity and that there are lots of allies and friends to help you along the way.

If your school doesn't have a gay-straight alliance, and you feel your school might benefit from one, look online for information about starting one. These kinds of clubs help to unite students, create a safe space to talk about issues, and build awareness within the school and community.

SCHOOL RULES AGAINST BULLYING

• We will not bully others.

• We will try to help students who are bullied

• We will make it a point to include students who are easily left out.

• When we know somebody is being bullied, we will tell an adult at school and an adult at home.

Gay-straight alliances can help establish rules for keeping you and your classmates safe.

A small number of people react to bullying by lashing out violently against their tormentors. They may fight with their bullies or become bullies themselves. In extreme cases, the target may feel so hopeless about his or her situation that he or she attempts suicide or, sadly, ultimately dies by suicide. In the aftermath, people who knew the bullied person often reveal that they were aware of the bullying but could not stop it.

PUSHING BACK AGAINST BULLIES

A growing awareness of all forms of bullying has led schools and even state governments to take steps against bullying. Antibullying or antiharassment laws are in place in much of the United States. However, indirect bullying, like social alienation, is difficult to stop because it is mostly verbal and a lot of it can take place outside the classroom.

Many students are able to overcome bullying. Some go on to help others do the same. One such student is Blake Graham, who was bullied by his peers at his high school in Pawleys Island, South Carolina. Blake was isolated by people who mocked the way he dressed, talked, and acted. He learned to deal with the alienation, then decided that he wanted people to like him.

Blake changed the way he ate and began exercising. He lost weight and gained confidence. He began working hard to get good grades and dedicated himself to helping others in his community. He became involved in many activities and programs at his school. He wrote two antibullying books for teens to show the harmful effects of bullying. As a teen ambassador for the national antibullying program Stomp Out Bullying, he works to educate others about the consequences of bullying.

During an appearance on a TV talk show in June 2011, singer and songwriter Taylor Swift spoke about being a victim of bullies when she was twelve and throughout her teens. She wrote the song "Mean," on her album *Speak Now* (2010), to bring awareness to the bullying issue and help others who have had similar experiences to build self-confidence. She has said that she often felt isolated by peers when she was in school. What helped her get through it was that she knew she could write a song later to express her feelings. Even in her career as an adult, she's continued to face bullying behavior. In 2017, the singer got into an online feud with TV personality Kim Kardashian when Kardashian released an audio recording of

Pop star Taylor Swift has opened up in the past about her personal experiences of being bullied.

Swift's voice sounding rather unflattering. Rather than retaliating, Swift dropped off social media for a while and then came back with a brand-new album a few months later. Many fans appreciated her positive approach.

Caitlin Uze has visited many schools to speak about how she was bullied as a seventh grader. As described in the *Martinsville Bulletin*, Uze said that when she was young, she wore eyeglasses and braces, and she talked with a lisp. As Miss Virginia in 2010, Uze traveled around the state to speak frankly to middle and high school students about the dangers of bullying and how she worked with a speech therapist to improve her public speaking abilities. Although she still speaks with a bit of a lisp, she believes that it is not how you say something but what you have to say that counts. Both she and Swift offer stories of hope in beating bullying. "It's about going out of your way to be kind and compassionate," said Uze in one speech to students.

Many organizations and programs work to curb or stop bullying. One of the most prominent programs is Dan Savage's It Gets Better Project. Savage and his husband, Terry Miller, launched the online video project in September 2010 in response to suicides by teens who were bullied because they were gay or because their peers suspected them of being LGBTQ. Since it was launched, more than sixty thousand people of all sexual orientations from all over the world have shared their stories. Many celebrities contributed to the project and its encouraging message that "it gets better." The project is still going strong years later, working to educate communities and stand up against prejudice.

The Council for Unity takes a more traditional approach to reducing bullying and violence in schools and communities. Since its founding in 1975, the group's hands-on methods have provided training to teach teens how to be responsible leaders in school and outside the classroom. The group also uses the arts—including painting and theater—to reenforce its curriculum. The group works to reach one hundred thousand young people from the ages of eight to twenty every year.

During Barack Obama's presidency, his administration launched its own antibullying initiative. The Obama administration developed the website StopBullying.gov as a way to provide information on how young people, parents, teachers, and others can work together to stop bullying. Obama made a video for the It Gets Better Project, along with members of his administration. At the press conference, President Obama talked about being teased when he was young because of his ears and his unusual name. He told the audience that bullying can have destructive consequences for young people. First Lady Melania Trump launched her "Be Best" initiative in 2018 to help combat bullying, urging young people to "encourage everyone to be kind to each other and treat each other with respect in everyday life and on social media."

The work of these people and groups has raised awareness of all forms of bullying. More people now understand that social alienation is a serious problem. They also know that there are more places for people who are targets to go for help in beating bullies and making friends. With luck, even more people will be able to put their bullies behind them and look to a bright future.

Middle school counselor DeAnna Edwards hugs a student on Blue Shirt World Day of Bullying Prevention.

GLOSSARY

ABUSIVE Extremely hurtful and insulting; engaging in violence and cruelty.

ALIENATE To cause someone to feel isolated or cut off from others.

ALIENATION The state of being an outsider or of feeling isolated, as from society.

ANONYMOUS Without any name acknowledged.

ANXIETY Distress or uneasiness of mind caused by fear of danger or misfortune.

BULLY A person who hurts, persecutes, or intimidates others.

BYSTANDER A person present but not involved in something.

DEPRESSION A mental condition marked by persistent gloom, feelings of inadequacy, and the inability to concentrate.

INGRATIATE To bring oneself into favor with someone by flattering or trying to please the person.

INITIATIVE The act of taking charge before others do; the ability to start things independently.

PASSIVE Unresisting to external forces or influence.

PEER A person who is equal to another in age, background, qualifications, abilities, and other categories.

SUBTLE Not immediately obvious.

SUICIDE The intentional taking of one's own life.

FOR MORE INFORMATION

BullyingCanada
27009-471 Smythe Street
Fredericton, NB E3B 9M1
Canada
(877) 352-4497
Website: http://www.bullyingcanada.ca
Facebook and Twitter: @BullyingCanada

BullyingCanada is a website created by young people who speak out about bullying and work to stop it.

National Bullying Prevention Center
PACER Center, Inc.
8161 Normandale Boulevard
Bloomington, MN 55437
(800) 537-2237
Website: http://www.pacer.org
Facebook: @PACERsNationalBullyingPreventionCenter
Instagram: @pacer_nbpc
Twitter: @PACER_NBPC

This center is committed to building awareness about bullying in useful and creative ways.

National Crime Prevention Council
2614 Chapel Lake Drive, Suite B
Gambrills, MD 21054
(443) 292-4565
Website: http://www.ncpc.org
Facebook: @McGruff
Twitter: @McGruffatNCPC

The National Crime Prevention Council provides resources on dealing with bullying.

Safe & Humane Schools
Clemson University, YFCS
321 Brackett Hall
Clemson, SC 29634
(864) 656-6712
Website: https://olweus.sites.clemson.edu
Facebook: @olweus
Twitter: @OBPPClemson

The Olweus Program's goals are to reduce and prevent bullying problems among schoolchildren and improve peer relations at schools.

StopBullying.gov
US Department of Health and Human Services
200 Independence Avenue SW
Washington, DC 20201
(877) 696-6775
Website: http://www.hhs.gov
Facebook: @StopBullying.gov
Instagram: @stopbullyinggov
Twitter: @StopBullyingGov

The US Department of Health and Human Services works to protect the health and well-being of US citizens. In a partnership with other US government agencies, this website (http://stopbullying.gov) provides information about bullying, what to do to stop it, and where to go for help.

The Trevor Project
PO Box 69232
West Hollywood, CA 90069
(310) 271-8845
Website: https://www.thetrevorproject.org
Facebook: @TheTrevorProject
Instagram: @trevorproject
Twitter: @TrevorProject

The Trevor Project is a national organization dedicated to crisis intervention and suicide prevention services for LGBTQ individuals under the age of twenty-five.

41

FOR FURTHER READING

Craft, Jerry. *New Kid*. New York, NY: HarperCollins, 2019.

Dawson, Juno. *This Book Is Gay*. Naperville, IL: Sourcebooks, 2015.

Halloran, Janine. *Coping Skills for Kids Workbook: Over 75 Coping Strategies to Help Kids Deal with Stress, Anxiety and Anger*. Eau Claire, WI: PESI Publshing & Media, 2018.

Hemmen, Lucie. *The Teen Girl's Survival Guide: Ten Tips for Making Friends, Avoiding Drama, and Coping with Social Stress*. Oakland, CA: Instant Help, 2015.

Jennings, Jazz. *Being Jazz: My Life as a (Transgender) Teen*. Toronto, ON: Ember, 2017.

LaCour, Nina. *Hold Still*. New York, NY: Penguin, 2019.

Mardell, Ashley. *The ABC's of LGBT+*. Coral Gables, FL: Mango, 2016.

Mayrock, Aija. *The Survival Guide to Bullying: Written by a Teen*. New York, NY: Scholastic, 2015.

Raja, Sheela, and Jaya Raja Ashrafi. *The PTSD Survival Guide for Teens: Strategies to Overcome Trauma, Build Resilience, and Take Back Your Life*. Oakland, CA: Instant Help, 2018.

Siwa, JoJo. *JoJo's Guide to the Sweet Life: #PeaceOutHaterz*. New York, NY: Abrams, 2017.

Skeen, Michelle, and Kelly Skeen. *Just as You Are: A Teen's Guide to Self-Acceptance and Lasting Self-Esteem*. Oakland, CA: Instant Help, 2018.

Soerens, Matthew, and Jenny Hwang. *Welcoming the Stranger: Justice, Compassion & Truth in the Immigration Debate*. Westmont, IL: IVP, 2018.

Toner, Jacqueline B., and Claire A. B. Freeland. *Depression: A Teen's Guide to Survive and Thrive*. Washington, DC: Magination Press, 2016.

BIBLIOGRAPHY

Anderson, Monica. "A Majority of Teens Have Experienced Some Form of Cyberbullying." Pew Research Center, September 27, 2018. http://www.pewinternet.org/2018/09/27/a-majority-of-teens-have-experienced-some-form-of-cyberbullying.

Corcione, Danielle. "How to Find a Therapist When Your Parents Won't Help." *Teen Vogue*, August 29, 2017. https://www.teenvogue.com/story/how-to-find-therapist-parents-wont-help.

González-Ramírez, Andrea. "Family Says 9-Year-Old McKenzie Adams Died by Suicide After Being Bullied." Refinery29, December 12, 2018. https://www.refinery29.com/en-us/2018/12/219285/mckenzie-adams-alabama-suicide-9-year-old.

Heil, Emily. "'Be Kind to Each Other': Melania Trump Continues Anti-Bullying Campaign." *Washington Post*, October 23, 2018. https://www.washingtonpost.com/arts-entertainment/2018/10/23/be-kind-each-other-melania-trump-continues-anti-bullying-campaign/?utm_term=.da9d938409bb.

Kodjak, Alison. "Teen Bullies and Their Victims Both Face a Higher Risk of Suicide." NPR, June 28, 2016. https://www.npr.org/sections/health-shots/2016/06/28/483758572/bullies-and-their-victims-both-face-a-higher-risk-of-teen-suicide.

Konnikova, Maria. "How the Internet Has Changed Bullying." *New Yorker*, October 21, 2015. https://www.newyorker.com/science/maria-konnikova/how-the-internet-has-changed-bullying.

Kutner, Max. "Teen Suicide Is Contagious, and the Problem May Be Worse Than We Thought." *Newsweek*, October 19, 2016. https://www.newsweek.com/2016/10/28/teen-suicide-contagious-colorado-springs-511365.html.

Lorenz, Taylor. "Teens Are Being Bullied 'Constantly' on Instagram." *Atlantic*, October 10, 2018. https://www .theatlantic.com/technology/archive/2018/10/teens-face -relentless-bullying-instagram/572164.

Malick, Amy. "Study: Bullying Common Among Teens." ABCNews. Retrieved February 22, 2019. https://abcnews .go.com/Health/story?id=117495&page=1.

Mayo Clinic Staff. "Teen Suicide: What Parents Need to Know." Mayo Clinic, February 6, 2019. https://www.mayoclinic.org /healthy-lifestyle/tween-and-teen-health/in-depth/teen -suicide/art-20044308.

Morin, Amy. "8 Ways to Teach Teens Anger Management Skills." VeryWell Family, January 11, 2019. https://www.verywellfamily .com/teach-teens-anger-management-skills-2609114.

Rettew, David. "Teen Therapy Without Parental Consent." *Psychology Today*, August 9, 2017. https://www .psychologytoday.com/us/blog/abcs-child-psychiatry/201708 /teen-therapy-without-parental-consent.

Sheehy, Kelsey. "Parents May Be Teaching Teens to Be Bullies." *U.S. News and World Report*, October 10, 2012. https://www .usnews.com/education/blogs/high-school-notes/2012/10/10 /parents-may-be-teaching-teens-to-be-bullies.

Stanley-Becker, Isaac. "A 9-Year-Old's Family Says She Committed Suicide After Racist Bullying, Including Taunts of 'Kill Yourself.'" *Washington Post*, December 12, 2018. https://www .washingtonpost.com/nation/2018/12/12/year-olds-family -says-she-hung-herself-after-racist-bullying-including-taunts -kill-yourself/?utm_term=.7f19c55dfd6d.

Wiseman, Rosalind. "5 Things to Teach Your Teen About Bullying." NBC News, June 27, 2015. https://www.nbcnews .com/feature/my-kid-would-never/5-things-teach-your-teen -about-bullying-n383101.

INDEX

ABOUT THE AUTHORS

Pam T. Glaser is the author of a number of books for teens. She also volunteers for antibullying and social justice causes and lives in Omaha, Nebraska.

As a volunteer elementary school tutor and peer counselor in high school, Jason Porterfield witnessed many instances of social alienation and the pain caused by bullying. He is a journalist and writer living in Chicago, Illinois. He graduated from Oberlin College. He has written numerous books for young adults.

PHOTO CREDITS